MW01298089

Finding Beauty
IN MY BROKENNESS

C. K. TUTTLE

WESTBOW
PRESS®
A DIVISION OF THOMAS NELSON
& ZONDERVAN

Copyright © 2021 C. K. Tuttle.

All rights reserved. No part of this book may be used or reproduced by any means, graphic, electronic, or mechanical, including photocopying, recording, taping or by any information storage retrieval system without the written permission of the author except in the case of brief quotations embodied in critical articles and reviews.

This book is a work of non-fiction. Unless otherwise noted, the author and the publisher make no explicit guarantees as to the accuracy of the information contained in this book and in some cases, names of people and places have been altered to protect their privacy.

WestBow Press books may be ordered through booksellers or by contacting:

WestBow Press
A Division of Thomas Nelson & Zondervan
1663 Liberty Drive
Bloomington, IN 47403
www.westbowpress.com
844-714-3454

Because of the dynamic nature of the Internet, any web addresses or links contained in this book may have changed since publication and may no longer be valid. The views expressed in this work are solely those of the author and do not necessarily reflect the views of the publisher, and the publisher hereby disclaims any responsibility for them.

Any people depicted in stock imagery provided by Getty Images are models, and such images are being used for illustrative purposes only. Certain stock imagery © Getty Images.

Scripture quotations marked NIV are taken from The Holy Bible, New International Version®, NIV® Copyright © 1973, 1978, 1984, 2011 by Biblica, Inc.® Used by permission. All rights reserved worldwide.

Scripture quotations marked NLT are taken from the Holy Bible, New Living Translation, Copyright © 1996, 2004, 2015 by Tyndale House Foundation. Used by permission of Tyndale House Publishers, Inc., Carol Stream, Illinois 60188. All rights reserved.

Scripture quotations marked TPT are from The Passion Translation®. Copyright © 2017, 2018 by Passion & Fire Ministries, Inc. Used by permission. All rights reserved. ThePassionTranslation.com.

ISBN: 978-1-6642-4952-3 (sc)
ISBN: 978-1-6642-4953-0 (hc)
ISBN: 978-1-6642-4951-6 (e)

Library of Congress Control Number: 2021923125

Print information available on the last page.

WestBow Press rev. date: 11/24/2021

Contents

Introduction

I am broken. There is a piece of me that will never be the same. I spent a total of twenty-one days in behavioral hospitals one fateful summer. I had to start seeing a psychiatrist at the age of thirty. At first, I was ashamed and wondered how I ended up there. I felt as though I should be able to handle the stresses of daily life like all the other moms, but instead I was diagnosed with bipolar disorder. The chemicals in my brain had decided to play tricks on me. I had a new identity, an ugly label, and a nagging self-judgment. I felt like my life had shattered, and it would never be the same.

"But he said to me, 'My grace is sufficient
for you, for my power is made perfect

in weakness.' Therefore, I will boast all
the more gladly about my weaknesses,
so that Christ's power may rest on me."
2 Corinthians 12:9 (NIV)

God's promise in 2 Corinthians helped me understand
that my weakness and my brokenness could bring me
closer to Him. It took time for me to find myself again
and come to grips with my new normal: the meds, the
counseling, the stigma. But God's grace was sufficient.
His power was truly made perfect in my weakness. He
started giving me the courage to share my testimony in
small group settings. He proved over and over that my
story was offering hope to others. I could feel God's love
flowing and moving through me, like a vessel for His
kingdom. I knew that it couldn't end there. He wanted
me to do more.

Dear reader, it is out of obedience to my Lord and
Savior that I write this book for you. My prayer is that it
will offer some type of encouragement to those who might

be suffering in silence. You are not alone. Whatever battles you face today, you have a God with an overwhelming, never-ending, reckless kind of love for you. It is my hope that my story will show you a glimpse of His faithfulness. Through my story, I hope you experience the miracle of how God pulled me out of a messy pit, and how He continues to give me strength to press ahead. I will offer tools that help me fight life's daily battles, and I will share scripture that speaks truth and empowerment into my life. Through my brokenness, I have found beauty. God created me in His image, and I will use my brokenness as an ember to ignite hope in this dark world. I will turn my mess into a message of the redeeming power of His love. Keeping my story to myself simply seems selfish, because my Almighty Savior deserves to be praised for all He has done.

> "Give thanks to the Lord and proclaim his
> greatness. Let the whole world know what
> he has done. Sing to him; yes, sing his

praises. Tell everyone about his wonderful deeds. Exult in his holy name; rejoice, you who worship the Lord. Search for the Lord and for his strength; continually seek him. Remember the wonders he has performed, his miracles, and the rulings he has given, you children of his servant Abraham, you descendants of Jacob, his chosen ones." Psalm 105:1–6 NLT

Chapter 1

POSTPARTUM PANIC

"I'm having a heart attack!"

This is what I shouted across the parking lot of Stein Mart as I slowly sat down on the hot summer pavement. "Sir, can you help me?" I yelled at a passerby. Luckily, this Good Samaritan stopped to help me inside the store. A few more beautiful souls brought me cold water to drink and dialed 911. They used my cell phone to contact my husband, and everything else was a blur. Before I knew it, I was being wheeled into the back of an ambulance and driven to the hospital. It quickly became clear that what I had suffered was not a heart attack. I had just experienced a panic attack that was out of this world.

To pinpoint the source of my anxiety was simple: I was a new mom, and I had two kids under two years old. The sleep deprivation, diaper dances, and feeding frenzies had put me in a tailspin. On this fateful day, I hit my breaking point. Rock bottom. I reached the end of the rope of the normal amount of anxiety that all mothers have. All rational thinking had flown out the window. In fact, I was such a basket case that I was in no shape to be released to go home. I was checked into a behavioral hospital. Also known as a psychiatric ward.

How did I get to this point? It's a long story. Let's go back to the very beginning, so you can get to know me a little better.

Looking back on my childhood, I remember being a bit of a perfectionist, and it was difficult for me to adapt when thrown into unfamiliar situations. I would thrive most with structure and routines. Maybe that's why I always enjoyed school. I don't remember being overly stressed about life, and although I'm sure I had typical worries, they never built up to a point that I lost myself in them. God blessed me with loving parents who provided a stable and supportive home life. Mom and Dad led by example and were always serving at church in some capacity. In fact, church became like a second home to me, and I accepted Jesus as my Lord and Savior at a young age.

My best and most vivid memories were made during our family travels. We vacationed every summer in Colorado, which was a beautiful relief from the Texas summer heat. Eventually, we had a group of eight families that caravanned with us on this most beloved trek. Making memories with these friends were some of the best times of my life. One set of grandparents had a farm in Tyler, Texas, and my other set of grandparents had a ranch in Zephyr, Texas. We frequently took weekend trips to both places, and George Strait was always the first playlist of choice on the road. I grew up around horses, and I always loved spending time outdoors.

I worked hard in school, and I was competitive about grades. I played volleyball and tennis in junior high, but I much preferred to be on the sidelines watching and cheering for others who were competing. Cheerleading became my sport of choice in high school. I lived for Friday nights under the lights of the stadium. The sound of the marching band (and our awesome drum line) brought excitement and joy to my small, simple teenage life. My love for choreographed dance started in this cheer squad.

My husband and I grew up together in church, and we started dating the summer before my senior year of high school. We got married at the ripe young age of twenty-one. If you believe in soul mates, then you could definitely put us in that category. Don't get me wrong; our relationship is not perfect. But I honestly believe that God handpicked this amazing man just for me. After I got married and graduated from college (yes, in that order), I became a middle-school math teacher. I had a passion for all things math, education, and middle schoolers. Not many people share this passion with me. I came across many who would wince and be baffled by my career choice. "Middle schoolers? Really? You like them?" The truth is I had a teacher/coach in middle school who made a huge impact on me at that impressionable age, and I wanted to give back in the same way. I wanted to be the teacher whom kids could confide in and talk to, because preteens begin pushing their parents away. My timid personality didn't lend itself to becoming a strict teacher, so it did take me a couple of years to find my "teacher voice." Once I figured out how to build a rapport with my students and motivate them to learn, it was somewhat smooth sailing. I knew I was meant to be in the classroom—at least for that season of my life.

All these blessings kept piling up, and I would frequently look at my life and think, "This is too good to be true. Something bad is bound to happen to me soon." But then I would go on my merry way and determine to be thankful.

In June 2011, my blessings multiplied tenfold when our first child was born. He was beautiful and, most importantly, he was healthy. At the time, I just assumed that I could balance my full-time teaching career with motherhood. I watched everyone else juggle it; how hard could it be? So, I went back to work exactly six weeks after he was born. However, I was not prepared for my heart to be torn so badly. As I tried my best to nurse (and pump) to provide what I thought was best for him, I wore my body out completely. I remember falling asleep at night on the couch with him in my arms, all cuddled up. I felt so bad that I hadn't seen him all day. I just wanted to spend every waking and sleeping hour with him when I got home from work. Eventually, any time that was spent away from him became torture. I couldn't understand why I had chosen to prioritize other children (my students) over my own child. Of course, this was irrational thinking, because all working mothers are providing financially for their own children.

One weekend, I decided to take my son to the park

and meet up with a friend who had a baby about the same age. We enjoyed the beautiful day together, and we decided to sit down in the grass and chat while our babies sat right in front of us. We got to talking, and before I knew it, my son started coughing and making a choking noise. My first thought was, *He must've picked up a stick or a leaf and tried to eat it without me seeing!* I grabbed him, stood up, and panicked. My friend took him from me and started the Heimlich maneuver as she had been coached. His face went from red back to normal in a matter of seconds, but those seconds felt like hours. That memory is forever etched in my brain. It rocked my world as a new mom, and I felt so guilty for taking my eyes off him and "letting that happen." I felt like a horrible mother. I felt like I had almost lost my son in that moment. I was so thankful for my friend and her swift rescue. I was so ashamed and scared from the incident that I hid this story from my husband, because I wanted him to trust me as a good mom. This experience triggered something in my brain that caused me to start to crack. Imagine a fragile glass heirloom that sits atop your mantle. One day you walk by and notice a small crack. You are upset, but you try not to be too upset because it's still intact and beautiful. This was me. I was doing my best to cover the crack in my own strength. I thought I could fix it. You know, a little super glue does the trick, right?

A few weeks later, one of my sixth-grade students came to me with tears in her eyes and told me that her best friend was threatening to commit suicide. I must admit that I panicked. I found the school counselor as fast as I could. The training I had received for situations such as this did not prepare me for the overflow of emotions that flooded in. This was the second incident where death became so real to me, and life seemed so delicate. My anxieties, worries, and fears about losing a loved one (or a student) were amplified. I became so horrified at the thought of losing someone that I could not go into work the next day. I tried getting up, getting dressed, and getting my son to daycare. I made it to school only to march straight into the counselor's office for talk therapy for myself! Luckily, I had a student teacher that year, and she was able to substitute my classes at the last minute. I went home for the day. I needed some time to regroup and pull myself together.

I had this gut feeling that I wasn't even in the right frame of mind to pick my son up from daycare until I first took care of myself. I splurged and went to the spa for a facial. (News flash! Spending money frivolously that you wouldn't normally spend is a sign of mania in bipolar patients.) My brain was not functioning clearly. There is no telling what my energy levels were, but I'm guessing they were slim to none. My student teacher became my saving grace. She picked up my slack, even on the days that I did make it to school. My sweet colleagues reached out and offered words of encouragement and hugs. But, y'all, I was in uncharted territory that I had never encountered before. I couldn't even put my makeup on in the mornings. (This was not like me at all.) I'm not sure what my students witnessed or wondered about me, but I must've looked like a zombie to them. There were class periods that became so difficult that I ended up in a conference room while my student teacher continued to take the lead.

By this point, I felt as though I was spiraling out of control. The perfectionist in me was so disappointed that I couldn't be the wife, mom, and teacher that I so desperately wanted to be. Remember the picture of the fragile glass heirloom atop the mantle? A nice, slow crack began to form right down the middle. I resigned my position at the school in April. And in Texas, that's right before the almighty state testing (the standardized tests that our teachers and students feel much anxiety about). The guilt of this decision was heavy on my heart, but I knew that I had to put myself and my family first for things to get better. For some reason, I did not seek professional medical help. I thought that staying home and taking the big stress of teaching off my plate would be the answer. It helped for a while, but the bigger issue at hand would soon resurface.

Chapter 2

ROLLER COASTER
OF EMOTIONS

July 2012

My extended family met up for a week-long vacation at the beach. My son was now one year old, and he was transitioning to drinking real milk and eating more solids. Although I was excited about our trip, I was very anxious and worried. Looking back, the worries seem silly now. I wondered how he would eat, sleep, and play safely in the rental home we would all be sharing for the week. (The perfectionist in me started hindering my ability to be flexible.) What would I do without his crib, highchair, and all his toys? Would the house be "toddler-proof"? Would the grocery store there have the food he likes? Before kids, a beach vacation sounded relaxing and fun. As much as I was looking forward to this one, I was also wondering how it could be relaxing with a toddler to chase all over the place. And my definition of "fun" would need revamping.

I went into vacation with the wrong attitude. I think I also took my mom's help for granted. I thought, *I deserve a break from the demands of parenting*, so I took her up on her offer to stay back at the house with him while I went and lounged in the sand with everyone else. (This sounds so selfish, and I hate to admit that is exactly what happened.) I was not comfortable with the thought of him walking through the mosquito-infested grasses that led to the big open ocean under the bright sun that causes sunburn. (Side note: One of my greatest fears is drowning.) You have my permission to call me over-protective and irrational, because that's exactly how I was acting. Most parents would love to treat their children to a vacation like this:

teaching your children to build sandcastles and watching them play in the waves. What was my problem, right?!

The first few nights there, I couldn't sleep. I would be the first out of bed (at an ungodly hour), and I would journal. I enjoyed sitting on the patio, watching and listening to the ocean. I felt as if I were in God's presence. I could feel Jesus holding my hand as I walked along the beach. That feeling had its advantages and disadvantages, though. It was causing me to detach myself from the people around me. I was ignoring the demands of my toddler and letting others pick up my slack. I didn't realize that my sleepless nights were causing me to think, speak, and act irrationally.

One night, I excused myself from family game time and went upstairs to take a hot relaxing bath. I remember trying so hard to take deep breaths and simply enjoy the alone time. Suddenly, I started getting pictures in my head of the horror scene from the movie, *What Lies Beneath*. Michele Pfeiffer is soaking in a hot bath when her entire body goes numb, and she is unable to move.

The water starts to fill the tub to overflowing and she comes remarkably close to drowning. Luckily, Michele's character survives by moving her hand just enough to open the drain. When I was able to shake the scary scene from my head, I jumped out of the tub and headed right back downstairs to join my family.

Everyone in my family could see that I was acting strangely, and they were concerned about me. Out of love, they kept trying to guide me out of the funk I was in. None of us realized that my thoughts and actions were out of my control. The chemicals in my brain were up to no good. When I got home, things were rocky for a bit. I argued with my husband over things that were not actually happening. I accused him of things that were not true. My brain was literally making things up out of nowhere. My family and closest friends can attest to the fact that I was not myself, and I said things that made no sense. I was sinking into a pit of depression and confusion, wondering, "What is wrong with me?" I visited my OB/GYN specialist and asked questions about postpartum depression. She prescribed her general go-to medication for new moms. Luckily, before things went totally out of control, God intervened and made all my symptoms disappear for a bit. He blessed us with another pregnancy.

"Pregnant? So soon?" When this baby was born, my son wouldn't even be two years old yet. Although it was a surprise, we were extremely excited, because we wanted two kids, and we thought it would be great if they were close in age. With pregnancy hormones, all the symptoms of depression, restlessness, and irrational thoughts vanished. My brain balanced itself out. I was glowing and happy and had plenty of energy to keep up with my toddler while my body was growing another baby. I was especially excited when we found out it was a girl. I spent many hours praying over the bond I would have with my daughter. I had visions and dreams of raising her to find beauty in God's love and spreading joy to others. My creative juices flowed freely while I was pregnant. I got artsy and made a plethora of decor for her nursery, all based around a theme of beauty and love. I found two key

Bible verses to center it around, and my prayer was that she would appreciate the beauty that comes from within us. To this day, I still try to teach her that a beautiful heart is much more important than our physical beauty as the world promotes it. She was born the day after Easter in 2013, and I found so many parallels between the new life that Jesus offers and the new little life, in the form of a baby, I was given.

May 2013

Blessings were abounding as our little family transitioned from three to four. I was staying home full-time and able to give my full attention to motherhood. Big Brother absolutely loved his new little sister. When she was six weeks old, we decided to rent an RV and go camping in Arkansas. I was much more flexible with this vacation; in fact, my attitude was the exact opposite of the beach vacation of 2012. Maybe it was because it was not my first rodeo with a baby. Maybe it was because we could take all our equipment easily—you know, the portable crib and such. Plus, my body provided all her food! (It's pretty cool that God made it that way.) So, we set out on our first adventure as a family of four. I bought captain's hats for Big Brother and Daddy. I loved cuddling with both of my babies in the back bedroom while watching "Toy Story" over and over during the drive. Arkansas in May is absolutely stunning, and we enjoyed hiking and paddle boat rides.

However, there was an incident where my true colors—my inflexibility and anxiety—would rear their ugly heads again. One day, while both kids were napping, my mother-in-law offered to watch them so Hubby and I could go on a hike. We got to the top of Mount Magazine—the highest point in Arkansas—and it was a gorgeous view. We noticed the clouds were darkening, and we remembered the weather forecast about a storm rolling in. For some reason, we didn't heed the warning. Instead of turning back toward camp, we continued the trail ahead of us.

The trail we chose took us down the other side of the

mountain, and then we would have to walk the long road around the base of the mountain back to our campsite. When it started raining, I began to complain, but all we could do was keep going. When it started pouring heavily, my emotional meltdown began. Suddenly, I was worrying that the baby would wake up, need to eat, and I wouldn't be there to provide for her because we were stuck in a storm. We made it to a motel that was on the premises and had to duck inside for a bit, hoping the storm would blow through quickly. After realizing that it wasn't going to stop any time soon, Hubby convinced me to step back out into the monsoon and make the trek back to camp. To say I was agitated would be a huge understatement. This was not what I had signed up for when I happily said, "Let's go hiking!" The windy, wet walk seemed to take an eternity. I remember turning the whole experience into a metaphor while I was walking. I thought, *This is it. This is a sign that something major is about to rock our world. We have been so blessed—nobody has a perfect life—what is the big obstacle that we will have to hurdle? What challenge is coming?* These mumblings were not just in my heart, they also came out of my mouth. As any husband would, mine was getting frustrated with my bad attitude. "Why can't you just relax and have fun? A little rain never hurt anyone." I'm sure he thought my reaction and over-analysis was ludicrous. When we got back to camp and opened that RV door, my mother-in-law was panicked and crying. (Mind you, both kids were still fast asleep.) She had been worried about us, and she had been unable to reach the rest of the family that was hanging out in the other RV. Sounds silly, but seeing her in that emotional state made me feel much better—like my emotions were normal and ok. We hugged and made the best of the rest of our trip.

Exactly one month after the fateful hike through the storm in Arkansas, my life would change forever.

Chapter 3

A PERFECT STORM

June 2013

The month of June brings many exciting celebrations for my family: Father's Day, my husband's birthday, my son's birthday, and our wedding anniversary. Back to back to back. My wife-heart and momma-heart always long to make each of these celebrations special for the people I love. This particular year, my husband would be celebrating his thirtieth birthday, and I was feeling the pressure to make his day even more special than in years past.

I was also experiencing a minor physical health complication that had thrown me for a loop. There are many complex factors that led up to the day my "Storm of 2013" began. These stresses were also making me lose weight. I know most people would love to experience that side effect, but not me. I'm a petite person, and I love food, but my daily routine of feeding the kids and changing all the diapers and keeping up with nap schedules was causing me to put myself, and proper nutrition, on the back burner. I have a high metabolism (plus I was breastfeeding), so I needed a healthy number of calories to keep my energy levels and milk production up. My body was using the calories faster than I could keep them coming in. It was also summertime in Texas, so the heat was rising, and I wasn't staying hydrated properly. All these factors were slowly contributing to stir a perfect storm within my brain.

On my husband's thirtieth birthday, I hit rock bottom. I knew that I didn't feel right, so I called one of my best friends to come watch the kids so I could get out of the house and find some respite. All I remember from this outing is finding myself at my church, speaking to the sweet receptionist who took a message for the pastor to get back with me. I was seeking help but didn't know exactly where to turn. I shortly ended up back home, and my friend gave me some words of encouragement before she left.

Later that same day, I found myself needing help again. I was in a panic that I didn't have a gift for my husband, so I called my father-in-law to come watch the kids. While I was out shopping, I had my first legitimate panic attack. It felt like a heart attack. This is when I found myself on the ground in the parking lot of Stein Mart, yelling for someone to come help me. I remember the ambulance ride and saying some irrational things. It was an out-of-body experience. There were some scary few hours that day, but the doctors must've found the right sedative and my mom and husband were finally able to have a somewhat normal conversation with me. The doctor recommended that I check into a mental health facility. I didn't know how to respond at first. I do remember being scared, but I also remember thinking, "I can't go home like this to my babies! So … ok, yes. Whatever we need to do to make me better!"

The fragile glass heirloom within my soul had just been shattered into a million pieces.

My husband drove me from the ER to the behavioral health hospital next door. I was shivering, freezing, and my thoughts were spinning. I also had the worst headache I have ever experienced. I felt like I'd been hit by a truck. My loving husband told me that he would go home and pack some comfy clothes for me. The nurses also had to find a hand pump so that I could ween my body from milk production. I was shown to my room and introduced to my roommate. I don't remember her name, but her appearance and silence were a bit intimidating at first. We warmed up to each other over the course of the next few days. My first night there, I ended up in the craft room where adult coloring pages and crayons were set out. The only other person in there was a young man who reminded me of one of my cousins. He was nice, and we chatted a little as we colored. It was cathartic and soothing for my brain. I felt like we were kindred spirits of sorts. Interestingly, I never saw him again throughout the rest of my stay. It was as if God had sent an angel to ease my mind and bring peace to my heart for that first difficult night.

My first few days, I distinctly remember going through the breakfast, lunch, and dinner lines in the cafeteria and trying to find a place to sit after filling my tray. I started to notice an older lady who sat by herself. The other patients seemed to avoid her. I made the bold decision to go and sit with her one day, and it wasn't until I was seated that I saw the scars on her wrists. They were too numerous to count. It took my breath away for a moment, but then compassion flooded through me. I was saddened by the thought that she had struggled so much to find relief from emotional pain. I remember starting a conversation with this lady. We just made small talk, and I think a small smile crept upon her face by the end of the meal.

As the days crept on ever so slowly, I attended therapy sessions in different formats. One was with a counselor and was intended for small group discussion. Another was in the form of crafts, and they brought beads of all shapes and sizes for us to make bracelets. I also spent some time in silence in the main gathering space or on my bed. The silence soon became overwhelming as I started to overanalyze what was happening in my mind, and it just ended up spiraling more and more out of control with irrational thoughts.

While psychologists were providing talk therapy, my assigned psychiatrist was diagnosing medications for trial and error. Unfortunately, she started with something that my body completely rejected. After multiple doses of my first medication, I began experiencing side effects such as the inability to communicate verbally. It felt like my tongue was frozen and thoughts could not be physically formed into words. My thoughts were stuck in my head with no way out. At one point, I refused to take the meds when they called for me, and I ended up receiving a shot instead. I remember laying in my bed thinking that my life was ending, and I would be with Jesus in heaven soon. My brain was making me believe that I was physically dying. My husband can vouch for me on this, because at one point I called him to let him know that I felt like I was in purgatory. I even told him that it would be ok to pull the plug if I was ever in a coma-like state. I can't imagine what was going through his head as he listened at the other end of the line. He knew that I was not thinking rationally, and he tried his best to tell me that I was going to be ok. He came to the hospital during visitation hours every night. And every night when he walked in, I would run into his arms, sit on his lap like a child, and just relish being in his presence. About a year later, when we were reflecting about this deep valley experience, he told me I was almost unrecognizable at the time. He had been very scared that I would never be the same person that he married, and he was fully prepared to do whatever it took to keep our family intact and cope with a new normal— whatever that would look like.

One evening, my mom came during visitation. One afternoon, my childhood pastor came to visit and pray with me. They both kept a brave face and did their best to encourage me, but I know they must have left the hospital with a deep fear in their heart. After four days and no signs of healing, my husband demanded that I be moved to a different ward (or unit) within the hospital. He had come to find out there was a unit that held senior citizens dealing with loss and grief. He was able to convince the staff to move me there, and it was a much different environment.

Among the seniors was a younger girl that I connected with instantly. She claimed that she was an author and had published a science fiction novel. She was also into yoga, and she taught me a few techniques. I was able to calm my heart and find some peace, and to this day I still love yoga. We also made more jewelry, and I was beginning to feel a little bit more like myself. I made two incredibly special bracelets that I wore every day during my stay. One bracelet had my kids' names with hearts in between. The second bracelet had the word LOVE with my husband's name.

Three days later, my mom and husband made the decision to sign me out of the hospital against medical advice. The doctor did not feel like she had reached the best diagnosis and prescription for me yet. She wanted one or two more days to observe my behavior. However, those "one more day" phrases were occurring every day and turning into way too many days away from family. I needed to be back home with my husband and children. I needed the warmth of hugs and the comfort of home. This seven-day "retreat" had not seemed to help much. In fact, some might argue that it made matters worse. It had taken me away from my nursing infant and toddler. It had caused me to try medications that caused serious side effects. Despite the doctor's disagreement, and after much red tape and legal paperwork, she begrudgingly discharged me and sent me home with meds she thought would help.

I arrived home and hugged my babies like they had never been hugged before. I remember my son looking at me differently. He was apprehensive and he wouldn't respond to my saying, "I love you." It cut me deeply that he wouldn't say it back to me, but I also understood that he had just experienced some small form of abandonment. I mean, think about it: his mom had up and disappeared without so much as a goodbye for seven days. I know he was only two years old, and he probably has no memory of the horrific event. But to this day, I feel like he has a scar on his heart and that he might suffer from separation anxiety because of my ugly psychiatric episode.

As I tried to assimilate back into my family role and routine, I began to experience numbness in my hands and tongue. They would freeze up and completely quit functioning. One night I was trying to read a book to my son and I literally couldn't form the words with my mouth. That same night, as we sat down to dinner, I couldn't use my utensils. My mom jumped on the phone with my doctor and she said to stop taking the prescribed medications and take Benadryl for the next few days. The side effects vanished as the meds left my bloodstream, but unfortunately, we were back to square one.

Chapter 4

THE DIAGNOSIS

August 2013

F or the next two months, my life seemed to return
to normal. I gained my confidence back, and I went
through the motions of motherhood. My son did start
saying, "I love you" again, and I remember soaking up
every moment with my two little blessings. I was also
seeing a Christian counselor once a week. Talking through
my experience was extremely helpful. We covered every
corner of my childhood, my personality, and my closest
relationships. We talked about my panic attacks and tried

to pinpoint my triggers. Then one day, he told me that he thought he might have a diagnosis for me. I remember him asking, "What would you think if a medical doctor told you that you have bipolar disorder?" I responded enthusiastically, "That would be so helpful! Then I could actually start to understand what is happening and get the help and medication I need!" We talked about the stigma that comes with mental illness, and I started coming to grips with the fact that I may have to battle this for the rest of my life.

I highly encourage counseling. It was a great relief to be able to talk through things with someone who has knowledge and experience with mental health. It was such an unknown territory for me and my family at the time. Part of my problem was fear of the unknown and fear of a dependency on medication. My counselor explained that mental illness is just like a physical illness. We are blessed to be born in a time when there is new research and medications for such ailments. God has provided doctors to help us work these things out, and failure to seek this help can result in catastrophic relapse. A diabetic wouldn't put their life on the line by refusing necessary prescriptions. So why would someone with bipolar disorder?

I was on the brink of getting the help I truly needed when the sleepless nights started. The stresses of life had built up again, and my brain would not shut down at night. I'm unsure how many nights in a row I went without sleep, but it was becoming a major problem. Not only was it agonizing as the nights were so long and lonely, it was also taking a toll on the rational part of my brain. If you have ever experienced a series of sleepless nights, then you can relate; you can't think straight. Normal tasks became more difficult, and I couldn't focus on completing one task at a time. My brain would wander, or it would start to race. Another storm in my brain started brewing.

After about a week without sleep, I experienced another panic attack in the middle of the night. Hubby and kids were sleeping, and I found myself in our guest bedroom blogging or scrolling my Facebook newsfeed so as not to wake my husband. I'm not sure what triggered the panic attack, but my heart began to race and I felt (again!) as though I was having a heart attack. It was such a scary feeling, and I ended up dialing 911 on myself. Imagine Hubby's reaction when I woke him and told him who I had just called. He was very confused, to say the least. When the paramedics arrived, they had tons of questions. They handed me a boost protein drink, and we all agreed that I would seek professional medical attention in the form of psychiatry the following day.

My supportive family had done their research and found a more suitable hospital that was privately operated and offered Christian care. Unfortunately, it took a lot of effort for my family to convince me to go and check in. My irrational brain couldn't understand what was happening and why it was the best decision. I am so blessed to have a support group of family members who came together and intervened for my well-being.

While my husband packed a suitcase for me, my brother and sister-in-law came over to pick up my son. My mother-in-law was charged with helping Hubby drive me to the hospital, and my father-in-law would be babysitting my daughter. (My parents were living in South Carolina at the time.) I took a prayer walk around my house that morning, because I felt as though it was under a spiritual attack. I forced my family members to pray with me, because I thought some of their souls needed saving. I wore a bright pink fluffy robe and refused to take it off. (Mind you, it was August in Texas.) After checking in at the hospital and telling Hubby goodbye, I was completely out of sorts and hyperactive. My mind was imagining that horrible things were happening to my family members. I still felt like Satan was on attack, and I could not calm down enough to sleep. There were two nurses with whom I felt comfortable talking about my fears. I asked them if they would come pray over me while I tried to fall asleep. And they did! And I slept. (Side note: Medication and a shot of some kind accompanied those prayers. But it all worked together to help me find rest that evening.)

Over the next few days, I would slowly begin attending

all scheduled activities and therapy sessions. This facility was much more comfortable than my previous experience. They had a courtyard with scheduled outdoor breaks, and these were the highlights of my day. It's amazing what the sunshine can do for your mood! Since this facility was privately owned, they had Bibles and Christian self-help books lying around everywhere. They offered a worship service on Sunday morning in the cafeteria, hosted by a nonprofit organization. The leaders shared their testimony, and it really hit home with me.

I carried a Bible, my journal, and a few books with me at all times. My Bible gave me comfort and provided truth when I needed it. My journal gave me an outlet to scribble all my emotions. I could also relate to the patients in this facility more easily. In fact, I made friends quickly, and we would share our stories with each other. At one point, I felt like I was at church camp. As I continued my daily routine and followed the appointed daily schedule, I started to wonder when I would be released to go home. I was feeling better. I took my meds at the appointed times and sat in for a quick checkup with the psychiatrist when he was on campus. I was doing everything "right."

I can't remember exactly how many days I had been there when I started to get the opposite feeling. It no longer felt like church camp. It started to feel like a prison. Suddenly, everything in me was fighting the system and trying to find a way to escape. I needed to get home to my babies, my husband, and my life. I even went so far as to call 911 from the hospital. This outlandish attempt got the attention of the staff, and I'm fairly sure they tried to ban me from going outside during the scheduled courtyard breaks. (Like I was going to try and climb the stone wall that surrounded it?) I must have convinced them to let me back outside, because I remember sitting at the table closest to the door from then on.

I can remember some of the faces of the people I met: An older gentleman who had just lost his wife. A mom in her 40's who had overdosed on pills. People seeking rehab for drug and alcohol addictions. I also remember the Bible-based therapy sessions where we would all gather to get these issues out in the open and battle our way through whatever hardship had come our way. Once I realized that it was a requirement to comply and work through the entire program before a discharge was even considered, my attitude changed. I quit trying to escape and started working to prove to the nurses, therapists, and doctors that I was on the mend and getting back to my normal self. After twelve long days, the doctors finally had a proper diagnosis for me! Bipolar disorder: the same diagnosis that my Christian counselor had guessed it would be.

Two medications were proving to be the correct chemical balance I needed, and I was finally released to go home. I remember the drive home from the hospital very well. I felt out of sorts, and I had to mentally prepare myself to step back into "my life."

Behind the Scenes

Thankfully, during both of my hospital stays, my mom was able to fly to Texas (from her South Carolina home) to stay with my family. She took care of my children so that my husband could keep working and visit me at night. What a blessing! She has always been the type of person who pours her heart into others with her words and actions. She is a fearless woman of God who is quick to make sacrifices for her loved ones. I want to put myself in her shoes for a moment and imagine what it must have been like for her during these horrifying summer months of 2013.

First, she gets a phone call from across the country that her daughter has been transported to the ER. Then, she listens to the doctor's recommendation and helps my husband make a really tough decision; they choose to check me into a behavioral hospital. She frantically packs her bags and jumps on the first flight to Texas. When she gets there, she is met by her tiny grandchildren who want and need their mommy. She does the best she can to explain where mommy is and comfort them. Then she starts to provide for their every need, including giving bottles and formula to a baby that had been nursing. All the while, she is wondering how her daughter is doing and praying for her mental health to return. Praying for doctors to make a proper diagnosis and get her on the proper meds. Praying for her daughter to return to the same girl she has always been, now a wife and mother to a little family that loves and needs her.

Mom told me that she had some friends in South Carolina that were prayer warriors. She told them the details of my story while it was happening, and they were praying for me. I also know that my closest family members and friends that knew of the situation were dialed in and talking to God daily on my behalf. And I now know, beyond a shadow of a doubt, that God had big plans for me to use this story to testify of His unfailing love. I felt His hand holding my hand while I was in the hospital. I could literally feel the weight of His truth as I carried those Bibles around the hallways of the hospital. I was drinking in His word like it was living water, and it provided the hope I needed in those dark hours. My mom said that one night when she came to visit me, I was able

FINDING BEAUTY IN MY BROKENNESS

to spout off chunks of scripture by memory like she had never heard me do before. My feet were planted firmly on my God. I was relying on Him to pull me out of that pit of mud and mire. I knew He could and would save me, but that didn't make it easy to wait. It was so difficult to be patient. I kept asking Him, "When?! When will I get to go back home, be with my husband and babies, and get on with my life?!"

Somehow, by the grace of God, I never lost hope.

> "Let all that I am wait quietly before God, for my hope is in him. He alone is my rock and my salvation, my fortress where I will not be shaken. My victory and honor come from God alone. He is my refuge, a rock where no enemy can reach me. O my people, trust in him at all times. Pour out your heart to him, for God is our refuge."
> Psalm 62:5-8 (NLT)

Chapter 5

MIRACLES

The summer of 2013 was the most terrifying, challenging, sometimes hopeless, dark, muddy, trying time of my entire life thus far. Still to this day, when I have flashbacks of that summer, I tremble. However ...

> "I waited patiently for the Lord; he turned
> to me and heard my cry. He lifted me out
> of the slimy pit, out of the mud and mire;
> he set my feet on a rock and gave me a
> firm place to stand. He put a new song in
> my mouth, a hymn of praise to our God.

Many will see and fear the Lord and put
their trust in him." Psalm 40:1-3 (NIV)

God put my feet back on solid ground, and He gave
me some awesome tools: a super supportive family, a
psychiatrist, and a counselor. I chose to continue seeing
the psychiatrist who first tried to help me in hospital #1.
We gave her all the new information from the doctors at
hospital #2, and she has done a fabulous job helping me
manage my meds these last eight years. Keep in mind
that the very first time she met me, I was "not myself"
and "unrecognizable." So, imagine her surprise when I
showed up to our first checkup appointment, looking
and feeling much more like myself. Her very first words
to me were,

"You are a miracle!"

A big smile came upon my face, and I almost started
laughing. Every time we meet, she asks me how I am
doing so well and remaining so stable. I always tell her

about my faith in my Lord and Savior, Jesus Christ, first. Then I mention my amazing support system of family and friends. I just keep hoping that one day she will want to know more about Jesus. I'm unsure of her religious affiliation. It never dawned on me until this very instant, as I type, to pray for her. For her soul, yes, but also for her practice. She helps many people who are struggling to find emotional and mental stability. She is on call 24/7. She is in high demand these days, and I wonder if that's the new direction of psychiatry. It seems as if the demand for mental health professionals is growing as new research continues to surface about our brains. I am so thankful for these doctors and the studies that are helping us find ways to manage disorders like mine.

A miracle. A medical doctor looked at me and
called me a miracle.

Now that I am eight years removed from the raw emotion of it all, I tend to take my health for granted on my good days. But I will never forget the word "miracle" and the new meaning it has for me and my family. Without God's powerful healing hand, I would still be stuck in the mud and mire. I would still be trying to pull myself out by my own strength. He provided the hospitals, nurses, doctors, medications, family, and friends that worked alongside me to pull me out. He provided a story about a miracle. He continues to provide for me when I find myself walking through another valley. He continues to lift me out of the pit when I find myself stuck. He wants you to know that you are not alone in your struggle either.

What are your struggles today? Maybe they are not related to mental health at all. But we all have struggles. Things that hold us back and strip us of all joy. Things that leave us questioning God's goodness and mercy. I'm here to tell you that those struggles do not have to define you or have power over you. Let me encourage you to pray for a release from those things. Pray that they would have no control over you. Lay them at the foot of the cross of Jesus today. He wants you to break free. He died so that you could be free from the sin, the hurt, the pain, and the suffering. He offers hope.

I am not completely healed. I will probably battle this disorder all my life. I have experienced setbacks, but God remains faithful. When I seek Him, He shows up. His love never fails. When I put my hope in Him, I can find peace and joy. It's not always easy. Joy does not always automatically bubble out of me, but I choose to continue to fight for it. In a later chapter, I will share some tools that have helped me navigate this daily battle against bipolar disorder. The work is not over. The pruning process is still in full swing. I will not reach perfection this side of heaven. God continues to teach me and refine me. He takes me through different seasons, and I have learned to simply trust the path He puts before me. I walk by faith, and not by sight.

After my homecoming from hospital #2, my memory is somewhat a blur. I remember that it took time to assimilate back into stay-at-home-mom mode, and I began regular checkups with my psychiatrist and continued regular visits with my Christian counselor. After some time, I did start to feel like my old self. I resolved to never, ever quit seeing my psychiatrist, and I was determined to follow her prescriptions very strictly. At the time, I thought I would never work outside the home again. I felt as though my experience and diagnosis would hinder me from holding a steady job. I tried not to worry about it too much since I was happy staying home to raise my children.

Two years later, God would prove me wrong.

Chapter 6

BACK TO THE
CLASSROOM

Summer 2015

When my son turned four, my husband and I started discussing preschool options. Big Brother had already spent two years in our church's preschool program, but we felt God calling us to take a tour of Covenant Christian Academy, a classical Christian school that offers pre-K through 12th grade. Financially, the only way it would be possible to enroll him was if I were receiving an employee discount. My husband mentioned the idea for me to apply for a teaching position. At first, the thought of going back to work scared me. *Would I remember how to teach a room full of teenagers? Would I still enjoy it?* I prayed about it, and I went ahead and turned in my application just to see what would happen.

I called a friend whose aunt was the middle school principal on this campus. I was hoping she could put in a good word for me. When I was called for my first interview, I was extremely nervous. First, I met with the elementary principal and headmaster. Their demeanor put me at easy very quickly. They were easy to talk to, and I was able to show them my portfolio and talk about my previous teaching experience in the public-school system. Once they realized that my specialty and preference was with older students, I was called back for a second interview with the middle school principal, the math department head teacher, and the academic dean. I have never had a more intimidating interview in my life. They quizzed me on my educational philosophy and how I would bring my faith into the classroom. "How can you use mathematics to teach children about God's love?" I was prepared to give them a lecture on best teaching practices and the strategies I had developed to reach all types of learners. Incorporating faith into curriculum was so foreign to me since that is obviously very taboo in public schools. Somehow, I was able to answer their questions with a small dose of confidence.

When I was called a third time, there was a job offer. Sixth grade math. It was my dream position! And it ended up being my dream job. I was able to follow my passion for teaching math while also having the freedom to teach about the love of God.

The next year, I moved into the seventh and eighth grade math position. I was able to teach some of the same students I had the year before, and we got to know each other even better. In fact, they were a little too comfortable in my classroom sometimes. They knew what I would put up with, and they knew that I wasn't a strict disciplinarian. (I had to reset some boundaries along the way.) Building a rapport with these students was so much fun. I was watching them grow into their adolescence, and I could see hormones changing as they were in my class for three years in a row. I invited seventh and eighth grade girls to eat lunch with me once a week, and we were able to talk about real life issues. I got to hear all about their passions, and we read some devotions together. I also coached the middle school cheer squad one year (another passion of mine). My two children attended the lower school, and I quickly became woven into the community. For three years, this school was my home away from home. I built meaningful relationships with these students, their parents, and my colleagues. I also had the flexibility of popping into my own children's classrooms during class parties or lunchtime.

I learned so much about myself during this time. I learned that my disorder did not define me. I really was still able to hold down a steady job. I was also able to share my testimony with a few parents whose children were struggling with depression and anxiety. We were able to connect on a deeper level, and I believe the parents were encouraged. I started feeling like my mental health journey had a higher purpose.

As good as it felt to be back in my comfort zone of the classroom, it also came with its challenges. I tend to pour my whole heart into my career. During my third year teaching in this caring community, stress started building up, and I felt my emotions tipping out of balance. My doctor helped me manage my medications, and we tried changing dosages, but we determined that the stress factor could only be relieved if I quit working full-time. My husband was super supportive, and we decided it would be best for me to refocus all my time and energy on my health and caring for our family. Resigning my teaching position was extremely difficult for me to do. I had made some meaningful friendships with colleagues, and I hoped and planned to keep in contact with them. My children would still be able to attend the lower school, and we would still be part of this community, but my personal position in it would drastically change. I would become one of the stay-at-home moms that had all the time in the world to care for myself and my family—or so I envisioned. I was excited about using my extra time to volunteer at the school and join the moms' prayer group.

It was a bittersweet day when I left campus for the last time as a faculty member. I felt as though my identity just kept shifting. Quick recap: After getting married, I was a career-driven teacher for seven years. Once I became a mom, I had trouble balancing motherhood and teaching. I resigned my job and transitioned to a stay-at-home mom. During this time, I had another baby and journeyed through a deep valley of panic attacks, hospitalizations, and a life altering diagnosis. A few years later, and feeling more like my old healthy self, I stepped back into the classroom to try my hand at becoming a working mom. I did love it for those three short years. But, alas, I found myself resigning again because it had become too much for me and my mental health. Can you imagine my heartache? Can you imagine the feeling of failure? I was right back where I had started. "Why, God? Why would you give me a passion for teaching and then rip it out from under me?" It was an easy decision when I got right down to it, because my health and my family were more important than a thriving career. That doesn't change the fact that I questioned everything. "Where do I fit in? What can I do to serve others outside my home? Something more part-time, perhaps."

Chapter 7

JESUS, JAZZERCISE,
AND JAVA

In May 2018, I packed up my classroom and walked away from my teaching position at our phenomenal school. I felt God calling me to rest. He was telling me to take the time to better serve my family and refocus on my health. My first area of focus needed to be my relationship with Him. I had always heard about the "Moms in Prayer" group at our school, so I decided to go and give it a try. After attending one meeting, I was hooked. This faithful group of women meets together once a week to share their testimonies and pray together. We pray for each other, for our children, and for the school community. We pray for people in our community with specific requests, and we watch in awe as God answers these prayers.

It didn't take long for me to open up and share my testimony with this group. These women came alongside me and lifted me up with such encouragement. They have walked with me through joyous times and dark times. They have prayed over me multiple times. In fact, this very group of women saw the vision and potential for this book. They became my biggest cheerleaders as I set out on this venture. They understood, more than anyone else, that it was a calling from the Lord. Their confirmation and encouragement made this book a reality. Because of this group, my prayer life was transformed from meek to powerful. God has given me a passion to go out, seek the hurting, and pray with them and for them. Since I have experienced the receiving end and been so uplifted, it is my turn to spread the light and lift others up. This courageous group of women has made a huge impact on my life. God is using them as a vessel for His kingdom.

I was thoroughly enjoying serving my family and spending more time with the Lord, but I also needed to get active and step back into a fitness routine. We all know that one of the best things for your mental health is exercise. Without hesitation, I headed to my favorite place to sweat it out: the dance floor at Jazzercise. I had tried many different types of workouts in my past, and this was by far my favorite. My history of cheerleading and my love of dance make this class more than just a workout for me, because it hits one of my passions. It's so fun! It's also an hour to break away from reality; an hour where stress melts away. Jazzercise is a dance cardio workout that incorporates strength training. It is also a community of women who encourage each other. Starting my day with a DanceMixx makes my day so much better. I leave class in a better mood, and I have more energy throughout my day.

Fast forward a few months, and God began opening doors for new opportunities. The first call was to become a Jazzercise instructor. Now, I say this was a "call" because the owner of the studio had been asking me repeatedly if I would be interested in getting my certification and joining her team of instructors. She will still tell you, to this day, that it took too many years to get me on board. But I finally felt like the timing was right, and after much prayer and discussion with my family, I chose to say yes. My love of dance was about to collide with my passion for teaching, and I was so excited to start something new and challenging. (And challenging it was!) For three months, my body and brain were working on overdrive to prepare for audition day. I changed my diet (more protein, please!) and was exercising more in one week than I ever had before (since those four years of high school cheerleading, anyway). Once I passed and was given my certification, I began teaching classes immediately. It was a little like being thrown to the wolves, I'm not gonna lie. I had to work even harder to create and practice sets of fifteen songs/routines for a one-hour class.

I have come full circle in this teaching career of mine. I'm back to lesson planning, modeling, teaching, and assessing, but this time I am teaching women of all ages. I still get a little nervous before each class, but the outcome and reward is so very worth it. I love watching my customers smile while they sweat! I love encouraging them to get the very most out of their workout, and challenging them to reach their personal fitness goals. I love the community of women there, made up of every age group and background, who come together for fun and fitness. More importantly, I love that we cheer for each other and celebrate each other's successes. I also love that we notice when a friend is having a difficult time, and we reach out to them. I love that nobody has to do this "hard thing" alone, and we hold each other accountable.

Group fitness is so much like life with God. It's so

much easier when we walk in community, alongside other believers, to encourage and lift each other up. With the Holy Spirit as our advocate and Jesus as our teacher, we know we can't go wrong. Jesus has modeled everything for us, but we must choose to "lace up and show up" (as my awesome Jazzercise friends like to say). We must choose to accept we are sinners, believe He died to save us from those sins, and commit our life to loving Him and making Him known. After that decision is made, and you're laced up, then you must show up and be ready to love others the way that He loves us.

I recently celebrated my two-year anniversary as a Jazzercise instructor. Now that I have some experience under my belt, I am becoming more and more comfortable memorizing new routines and cueing the choreography. I am also learning so much about physiology and the world of physical fitness. As I teach my classes with physical safety and fitness in mind, I also speak to my customers about our "mental fitness." Some of my favorite routines are kickboxing style, and I literally tell my customers to kick and punch their stress away. I remind them to leave all their stress at the door when they walk in, and focus on having fun as we dance. They should leave feeling better about themselves—like they can go conquer the world. Their endorphins should have kicked into high gear. Apart from the physical benefits of an exercise program like this, there are so many mental health benefits.

With every New Year, I love to make resolutions and set goals for myself. At the beginning of 2020, I decided to make it simpler. Instead of writing out too many lofty goals, I decided to choose one word that would encompass my mentality for the year. The word I chose was *courage*. It takes major courage to share this kind of personal story with you, my dear reader. I was questioned on many sides about whether this was a good idea. However, I was encouraged by many more people to continue this journey of opening up and sharing it. The Lord started tugging at my heart to do something else courageous. I felt the desire to get more personal with the women in my life. Sitting behind a computer screen and writing about my experience is not the same as sharing it with someone firsthand. I knew there were women out there needing connection, needing encouragement, and needing to know they are not alone in their struggles. I could see it in their faces. I wanted to reach out and get to know them better. We have so much to learn from each other, and I was sick of the small talk. I wanted more. But how?

The answer was simple: coffee. I started inviting friends and acquaintances out for coffee. One-on-one. I wanted to invest in my sweet sisters in Christ in a meaningful way, using the gift of time. (How often do we slow down long enough and take the time for meaningful conversation?) I wanted to listen to their stories and then share mine. I wanted to knock down walls of judgment, shatter the stigma of diagnoses like mine, and open doors for real, authentic communication. I wanted to encourage other women and pray over them. Little did I know that the Lord was setting me up to hear encouragement right back from them. In meeting with some super-sweet women whom God placed in my path, my eyes were opened to a world of things I was previously blind to. I heard personal testimonies that sent shivers down my spine. I often met with women who were older than me and had had more life experience. I was able to glean so much wisdom from them. These coffeehouse conversations have become my favorite pastime. When the kids are in school and an opportunity arises to meet up with someone whom God has placed on my heart, I go. We talk. We might laugh together, we might cry together, and we might pray together. Sometimes our conversation is easy and lighthearted. Sometimes we get into deeper topics. But every time, I leave the coffeehouse with a thankful heart and a renewed sense of peace. I am reminded that I am not alone. This journey of life is not easy, but we were never meant to do it alone! We were created to be in community.

Never once have I invested time in someone else and walked away feeling empty. In fact, I believe the more we give and serve others, the more God fills our cup to overflowing. When I get stuck in a rut and choose to stay on my couch, isolating myself from others, I fall victim to the "me" mentality. Suddenly I am complaining more, comparing more, and feeling like I don't measure up. I lose my joy and my zest for life, and I can't get motivated. But when I make the choice to show up to Moms in Prayer or Jazzercise, I get my joy back. Being around other people lifts my mood.

> "And let us consider how we may spur one another on toward love and good deeds, not giving up meeting together, as some are in the habit of doing, but encouraging one another." Hebrews 10:24–25 (NIV)

Chapter 8

ROAD TO REMISSION

Remission: a period of time during a serious illness when the patient's health improves; a temporary recovery; a diminution of the seriousness or intensity of disease or pain (*Merriam-Webster.com*).

I will never forget the day my psychiatrist described my disorder as being "in remission." I was elated to hear those words come out of her mouth, but I didn't quite understand what it meant. I still question if it is possible to be completely healed from something like this. I wonder if there will ever be a time in my future when I won't have to be dependent on medication to keep me stable. I do have relapses where I experience extreme highs and lows. That must be why the dictionary defines remission as a temporary recovery. It differs tremendously from the word "cure." If I was cured, then I would not need daily medication, and I would not be in jeopardy of experiencing manic episodes. I feel as though there will always be an underlying battle in my brain. The good news is that we can learn tools to help keep it under control where the intensity is diminished.

My greatest fear is that I will end up in the hospital again, unable to function and unable to care for my kids. For this reason, I made the decision to follow my doctor's orders and never stop taking my medication. This has been the best thing I could ever do for myself and for my family. It takes discipline to see a psychiatrist every four months, keep the medications refilled, and remain consistent to take them every night. This discipline has been one key to my success in finding peace and healing.

I would like to share a few other tools that have helped me remain mentally and emotionally stable. This is, by no means, a complete list. It is also unique to my personality and passions. We are all uniquely designed and created by God, so these may not work for everyone. However, some of these tools are research-based and have been scientifically proven to decrease anxiety and depression. I encourage you to read through my toolkit with a fresh perspective.

Tool #1: Faith

"Consider it pure joy, my brothers and sisters, whenever you face trials of many kinds, because you know that the testing of your faith produces perseverance. Let perseverance finish its work so that you may be mature and complete, not lacking anything. If any of you lacks wisdom, you should ask God, who gives generously to all without finding fault, and it will be given to you. But when you ask, you must believe and not doubt, because the one who doubts is like a wave of the sea, blown and tossed by the wind. That person should not expect to receive anything from the Lord. Such a person is double-minded and unstable in all they do … Blessed is the one who perseveres under trial because, having stood the test, that person will receive the crown of life that the Lord has promised to those who love him." James 1:2-8, 12 (NIV)

The battles we face each day come in many forms. I'd like to expound on the one I find myself in when my bipolar tendencies flare up. During these dark times, my greatest enemy is Satan and the lies that he tries to feed my brain. I begin to feel paranoid, and my fears become amplified. It becomes difficult for me to watch the news or violent tv shows when my mania sets in, because sad and scary events cause me to think that something similar is about to happen to someone I love. My brain plays tricks on me, and I analyze every interaction so much that I misinterpret conversations and take things personally when they weren't meant to be that way. Communication with my closest family members becomes very frustrating during these times. However, I have learned that my faith should be bigger than my fears. I have learned to call on the name of Jesus to cast out all fears and all lies of the enemy.

The first way to exercise your faith: arm yourself with prayer. Ask for the Holy Spirit to surround you, and ask for wisdom. You can also ask family and close friends to pray for you. The key takeaway here is this: open up about how you are feeling, and let others in. Hiding behind the shame and keeping your feelings inside will only make you feel lonely. And lonely can become a terrifying place to be.

The next best way to exercise your faith: open your Bible. Find passages that encourage and remind you that there will be deliverance and victory. Crank up the praise and worship music! Not only will you instantly find yourself singing, but many of these songs come straight from Scripture. The uplifting lyrics will make their way into your heart and equip you for the day ahead.

It may sound like the most clichéd Sunday School answers here—"Just pray, and read your Bible!"—but when is the last time you took those two things seriously? When is the last time you actually made time daily for both of these things? I still fall short. I know how important they are, and I still find myself making excuses for not taking time to sit with Jesus each day. Let's make it a priority. Don't put it off any longer. Today is never too late to start.

If you don't know where to start, Romans 8 is a great place:

> "...The Spirit helps us in our weakness.
> We do not know what we ought to pray
> for, but the Spirit himself intercedes for
> us through wordless groans. And he who

searches our hearts knows the mind of the Spirit, because the Spirit intercedes for God's people in accordance with the will of God. And we know that in all things God works for the good of those who love him, who have been called according to his purpose." Romans 8:26-28 (NIV)

These verses point out a few important things. If you don't know what to pray or how to pray, that's ok. The Holy Spirit has your back. He already knows how you feel. He hears your groaning and sees your pain. And all the pain you endure is working for good and for His purpose. We may never fully see or comprehend His purpose this side of heaven, but we must choose to trust it, or we will never find peace.

Tool #2: A Caring Community

God created us to live in community. It is imperative to find a support system for yourself. Mine consists of many different types of people in my life. I have already mentioned many of them: my doctors, my counselor, my family and close friends. I also briefly mentioned how important it is to open up to them in dark times. I cannot emphasize this point enough. When Satan's lies start to creep in and I begin to feel surrounded, I always try to hide it at first. I try to fake it; I put on a smile and pretend everything is ok. Sound familiar? I know I'm not the only one who does this. Now I know it's important to push through and "be strong"—especially for our children. But if we knew that someone we loved was crumbling on the inside, wouldn't we want to know? Wouldn't we want to reach out and offer help? That's exactly what your loved ones want to do for you. Fortunately for me, my husband can detect that something is "off" before I have the courage to admit it out loud. However, this is after years of living with bipolar disorder and reflecting on the situations that have triggered my past episodes. We communicate openly about how I am feeling and what might have been a trigger. Hubby knows me better than I know myself sometimes, and he is my greatest sounding board. He also encourages me to call my doctor when it seems necessary. His support has been crucial to my remission. Outside of family and close friends, I find my greatest support groups are the women at Moms in Prayer, Bible study, and Jazzercise.

Let me encourage you to *find your* support network. If you feel alone and you don't know where to turn, start by going to church. Find a church in your area that welcomes you with warm handshakes and smiles. Get to know the people there. Attend a small group. Volunteer. If that seems too overwhelming, then start small. Reach out to one person—maybe a co-worker—and invite them to coffee or lunch. As you get to know them better, be brave enough to open up to them. Go beyond the small talk. Share your story. I promise you will see amazing things happen. God will open doors for friendship and you will find that you are not alone in your struggles. I know it's risky to be vulnerable, and it's important to find people you can trust. But you can trust God in the process too. Ask Him to lead you to the right people.

I would be remiss if I didn't mention the importance of talk therapy and medicine. Psychiatrists, psychologists, and counselors are gifts from God. Seek them. Ask your friends for recommendations in your area. There is no shame in this. They are an integral part of your support system and caring community.

Tool #3: Exercise

The *Primary Care Companion to the Journal of Clinical Psychiatry* states, "Exercise improves mental health by reducing anxiety, depression, and negative mood and by improving self-esteem and cognitive function" (https://www.ncbi.nlm.nih.gov/pmc/articles/PMC1470658/). It doesn't get more cut and dried than that. If you do not have a regular workout routine, let me encourage you to find something that is right for you. You can start by simply walking. It's free, and you can be outside enjoying God's creation. There are all kinds of apps that can help you go "from couch to 5K" and amp up your game to jogging and running longer distances. There are so many workout programs to choose from these days. Find something that fits your passions, lifestyle, and budget. And, if there's a Jazzercise class near you, we would love to see you on the dance floor!

Tool #4: Journaling

> "A personal journal is an ideal environment in which to become. It is a perfect place for you to think, feel, discover, expand, remember, and dream."
>
> — Author Unknown

Journaling is a wonderful way to document the joys, sorrows, or battles of my life. It helps me organize my thoughts and beliefs. I love to take note of what I am learning through circumstances, sermons, or my time in God's word. It's amazing to go back and read something that I wrote in the past. I can see my personal growth, and

I can see the prayers God answered. Journaling is one of the great tools that helped me through my darkest times and continues to help me heal.

I started journaling before I had children. In fact, the oldest journal I have on hand is dated April 2010, and my very first entry is all about the fact that we were officially trying (and struggling) to start a family. I wrote about the things that were happening in my life, and I wrote about what the Lord was teaching me. I journaled thoughts and ideas and dreams of writing a book. It's funny looking back at it, because I had ideas of topics, titles, and chapters (none of which are part of this book). Nine days after my first journal entry, I started a blog. I'm not sure what prompted me to take my thoughts public and share them online. I guess I'm just wired to share and try to relate to others. I thought that maybe something I was learning in my time with God could help someone else out in cyberspace. Little did I realize the one person it was helping the most: me.

I posted forty-nine blog entries before my storm of

2013. And in the middle of the storm, I was journaling like you wouldn't believe. I mentioned before that I would carry Bibles and journals around the hospital during my stay there. I took pen to paper *daily*. My thoughts needed out. Looking back at those journals, some of my scribbles make sense and some don't. But at the time, those blank pages became a place for me to let all the feelings loose. They offered freedom. Upon returning home from the hospital that summer, I went into a sort of hiding. I had to spend some time figuring out who I was and how to move forward in living with the stigma of my diagnosis. I continued to journal, but I did not post anything on my blog during this time. I felt as though I had a new identity, and I most definitely had a new testimony. A new mission. A new story to tell.

Writing this very book has been extremely cathartic. Reflecting on God's goodness through my deepest valleys reminds me that He is always faithful. I encourage you to start a prayer journal. First, list everything you are thankful for. Then, list your prayer requests. This is a great way to start your daily journal entry. You will also be able to look back one day and see how God answers prayer.

Tool #5: Get outside (literally and figuratively)

According to *Business Insider*, research suggests that spending time outside can improve your physical and mental health (https://www.businessinsider.com/why-spending-more-time-outside-is-healthy-2017-7).

When I reflect on my time spent in the behavioral hospitals during the summer of 2013, I remember so clearly how a short visit to the courtyard would brighten my mood. For fourteen days, I was under lock and key inside a stuffy building while they observed my behavior and provided therapy sessions and therapeutic activities. One of the most therapeutic things they offered was a chance to get outside for fifteen minutes. One thing I love most in this world is travelling. When my husband and I get the opportunity to travel, we plan trips to places that offer the best scenery and outdoor activities. We don't care so much for the big cities; we prefer renting a car and driving through the countryside. When we were house hunting, we were in search of a place that offered the best possible backyard. When we drive around town at sunset, I am the first to point out all the beautiful colors that God has painted across the sky. I am in awe of God's creation, and being outside connects me to Him. It reminds me of His majesty, His power, and His promises. So first, I encourage you to literally get outside. Spend more time in your own backyard or at a local park. Find restaurants that offer outdoor seating when the weather is nice. And there's one more important rule here: No phones allowed. Take some time to get away from all that distracts you. Open your eyes to the beauty around you. Breathe it in. Enjoy the scenery, and find rest.

If you are a person who is always on the go, like me, then I pray that connecting with nature will also allow you to slow down. So, secondly, I encourage you to "get outside" figuratively. Let me expound. City life tends to bring a sense of chaos and busyness to our culture. We race around running errands and taking our kids from one activity to the next. We bury our heads in our phones. We see new trends and become tangled in the rat race of working harder so we can have more stuff. Our worldview becomes clouded with the desire for more, and we succumb to the need for instant gratification. Enter Amazon. The world at your fingertips. New stuff! Only the coolest, name-brand stuff! We must have all the stuff! I just had a profound thought: stuff rhymes with fluff. And that's exactly what it is. It's all a bunch of unnecessary fluff.

Step back for one moment with me. "Get outside" of that rat race, if you will. Reflect upon the last time this lifestyle offered you some peace. For me, it is the opposite of peace. Oftentimes, I crave rest from the rat race. I hate the comparison game. I hate the feeling that social media leaves me with sometimes, because I see all the pictures of other families doing "all the things." Things that my family doesn't do. As hard as I try to hit the "like" button and be happy for my friends, that evil spirit of jealousy is crouching around, just waiting to rear its ugly head.

But then, when I take a step back and look at my life, my husband, my children, our blessings, and the things that *we do* experience together, I'm reminded how silly the comparison game is. Let me encourage you to "get outside" of the game of life. Step into a new perspective. Life is not a game. It's a journey that we are privileged to partake in with the God who created us. He wants a relationship with you today, and He wants you to have meaningful relationships with others. Remind yourself of the blessings you have sitting right in front of you.

Chapter 9

SHATTERING THE
STIGMA

"**M**ental illness isn't a uniquely modern phenomenon. The genetic influences that stand behind some types of mental illnesses, along with the physical and chemical assaults that can spark illnesses in some people, have always been part of human life. But the ways in which impacted people are treated by their peers, as well as the help ill people might get from their doctors, has undergone a significant amount of revision. In fact, the ways in which modern cultures both understand and deal with mental illnesses have undergone a radical transformation. However, much work remains to be done, if people who have mental health concerns are to reach their true potential." —Foundations Recovery Network (https://dualdiagnosis.org/mental-health-and-addiction/history/)

If you've done any research about the history of mental health treatment, then you know how scary our past is. The words "insane asylums" and "loony bins" have never haunted me so much as they do now. It has only been since the 1940s that chemists began experimenting with powders and pills that could calm imbalances in the brain. And even with new medications to help us, there are still times when one might need to be admitted to a hospital for observation and different therapies until a diagnosis may (or may not) be correctly given.

After being discharged from my second hospital stay and receiving the right diagnosis, everything I thought I knew about myself vanished. I felt the weight of a new identity bearing down on me. *People will look at me differently. It will be difficult to get a job. Can I even hold a*

steady job? Can I be the mother I need to be for my children?
It took time and counseling to realize that this disorder
does not have to define me. I am still the same person
I have always been. I have a new challenge, but it's not
something to be afraid of. And I believe that I shouldn't
be afraid to talk about it either. Hence, the reason for
this book. I believe I went through this dark valley for
a reason. (Or maybe I just refuse to let it serve no good
purpose.) I am purposing to use my testimony for God's
glory. I will not back down and stay silent just so that
others think I'm "normal." I know it's not normal to tell
the whole world about your shortcomings, your secrets,
or the things that make you weak. But I have a God that
is so strong, and He wants you to know about His power.
I will be here to tell about it every day that I have breath.

My hope is that my faithfulness to testify and tell my
story will encourage others to do the same. We all have a
unique life story. We have different life experiences and
personalities. Different talents and strengths. Different
struggles and weaknesses. Different interests. I pray

that we will no longer fear those differences. I pray that they will not stop us from getting to know each other. I pray that those walls that separate us will come crashing down as we reach out in the name of Jesus to offer encouragement to each other. We should celebrate our differences and come together as one Body of Christ to serve Him and praise Him. My first step was to write this book. My second step was to begin inviting people to chat over coffee. Now more than ever, people are feeling lonely and isolated. Mental health struggles are on the rise. I'm only one person and I feel as though there's not much I can do to make a difference. However, Paul Shane Spear once said, "As one person I cannot change the world. But I can change the world of one person." This is where I will start. One small text. One small phone call. That's all it takes. Has God put someone on your heart today? Give them a call. Ask how you can pray for them.

"In your day of danger may the Lord answer and deliver you. May the name of the God of Jacob set you safely on high! May supernatural help be sent from his sanctuary. May he support you from Zion's fortress! May he remember every gift you have given him and celebrate every sacrifice of love you have shown him. May God give you every desire of your heart and carry out your every plan as you go to battle. When you succeed, we will celebrate and shout for joy. Flags will fly when victory is yours! Yes, God will answer your prayers and we will praise him! I know God gives me all that I ask for and brings victory to his anointed king. My deliverance cry will be heard in his holy heaven. **By his mighty hand miracles will manifest through his saving strength. Some find their strength in their weapons and wisdom, but my miracle deliverance can never be**

won by men. Our boast is in the Lord our God, who makes us strong and gives us victory! Our enemies will not prevail; they will only collapse and perish in defeat while we will rise up, full of courage. Give victory to our king, O God! The day we call on you, give us your answer!"

—Psalm 20 (The Passion Translation)

What an amazing picture of the victory we have in Jesus! King David's words are so powerful here. No weapon or wisdom that I have on my own can defeat the enemy. I find my strength in my Savior because He has already claimed victory. Time and time again in my life, I have experienced "miracles manifest through his saving strength." After each deliverance, I shout praises to Him! I have the desire to tell of His goodness and share my story. He gives me courage, and I am reminded that I am made strong in my weakness.

My prayer is that, together, we can claim this victory

we have in Jesus and begin shattering the stigma of mental health struggles.

Closing prayer:

Father, I come to You asking for wisdom.

Wisdom to know the next steps on shattering the stigma of mental health in our communities.

Wisdom for doctors in this field of expertise.

Wisdom for any person reading this who might be battling their emotions, and courage for them to say something to someone they love. Courage to seek professional help.

Wisdom for family members of someone who is struggling emotionally.

Father, I ask You to crush Satan and his lies under Your mighty feet. Arm us with Your word so that we are protected day and night. Keep us under Your mighty wing. Shine Your light and Your truth throughout our nation and throughout our world. We have victory when we place our trust in You, Lord. Give us hope. Give us new mercies every morning. Thank you for the work You will do in denouncing and shattering the shame of mental illness. It starts with one person. One tiny spark can light the fire. Help us band together, stand strong together, and walk through this decade together with You at our side.

As COVID-19 has rocked our world recently, I pray for healing. Physical and emotional healing. I pray that people would not be afraid to live their lives. I pray for any and all fears to be released and given to You. I lift all anxieties up to You, Jesus. Bear this burden for us just as you bore the cross. We thank You. We love You.

Amen.

Appendix

Online resource

Since 1949, our nation has observed Mental Health Awareness Month every May. If you visit <u>www. mhanational.org</u>, you will find a plethora of information to help you live a mentally healthy life. Some information includes Ten Tools to help you feel stronger and more hopeful. (www.mhanational.org/ten-tools) They outline easy steps you can take in each of these ten areas:

- Connect with others
- Stay positive
- Get physically active
- Help others
- Get enough sleep

- Create joy and satisfaction

- Eat well

- Take care of your spirit

- Deal better with hard times

- Get professional help if you need it

CPSIA information can be obtained
at www.ICGtesting.com
Printed in the USA
BVHW030249221221
624681BV00005B/175

9 781664 249523